MW01174508

Anywhere Is Home

poetry
by
Joanna Lawson

Serengeti Press

Published by: Serengeti Press
                  P.O. Box 1246, Station "B"
                  Mississauga, Ontario
                  L4Y 3W5

                  Stella Mazur Preda, Publisher
                  Jeff Seffinga, Editor

Cover Illustration by Kim Davis, Dundas, Ontario

Cover Design by Stella Mazur Preda

Lawson, Joanna: 1935 -
       Anywhere is Home, a book of poems

Canadian Cataloguing in Publication Data
1. Title

PS8623.A94A66 2005   C811'.6   C2005-901035-5

ISBN 0-9732068-7-X

Printed and bound in Canada by e-impressions inc.

Dedication

I dedicate *Anywhere Is Home* to Judi, Susan, and Jackie, at Jackie's Travel Agency in Ancaster, Ontario, Canada (905-648-8747). They arranged all the trips, handled any problems that arose through the incompetence of others and sent me on my way with smiles. They also listened to my debriefings when I returned. I write in the past tense but I am not through travelling and their work is not done yet.

Acknowledgements

I thank the members of Tower Poetry Society for all their thoughtful criticism through the years in our monthly workshops. I appreciate the efforts of my publisher to make these poems look presentable and error free. I thank my early mentors, my uncle Vincent Francis (1912-1989) and his best friend, Bill Moore, who continues to celebrate my successes.

Lastly, I thank Janet, Drake and Drina, my daughter and grandchildren, who look after my home and my cat(s) between travels. Dusty, my most recent housemate doesn't appreciate their efforts but I do. Without their willing help and unselfish support, I could not travel as worry free as I do. Dusty takes a few days to forgive me my absences but eventually celebrates my return.

CONTENTS

Mexico

USA

EUROPE

England

Ireland

Switzerland

France

Germany

Portugal

Spain

Norway

ASIA

Russia

Turkey

ON THE ROAD

Disney Music

Silence has ended.

After four days of joyful music
exuberant screaming children
death defying water slides
threatening giant waves
picture moments with Mickey,
rides and shows that elicit
roars of thunderous applause,
creative silence fills my head.

For four days no words
scrambled to be written,
no images struggled to be heard,
neither Typhoon Lagoon nor
Magic Kingdom nor Main Street
summoned the muse.

Now alone on MAGIC's promenade deck
as I watch waning white moon
and growing red sun, she
softly spills words into my ears.

CRUISING

Morning Sun on the *Disney Magic*

Awake, Awake
shouts the sun in joy

Her shimmers on the water
have called quietly
while she broke the horizon
to whisper her hello.

Now, she fills the sky
washes red across umbrella world
beckons the ship ever nearer
and turns sound of parting waves
into glorious hallelujahs.

Cruise Ship Isolation

On the deck the ship rolls
on laughing diamonds
of sensuous cobalt swells.
A sea orchestra fills the air
with myriad rippled murmurs—
sea and soul are one.

In the ship sculpted space
forms pockets of affable activity
dance   drink   gamble   talk.
Forgotten— silent blue world
beyond the window frames.

CRUISING

Pacific Ocean

Steeped in stories of huge hungry waves
today she emulates her name.
Our ship, cradled in her waters
rolls in sun sparkling waves
while our wake hums a lullaby.

Fierce winds are memories, or lurching in the wings
now breezes billow us north
We breathe lightly and stroll the deck
with feet wide apart—remembering
she was named in irony.

Reflections

Unexplored landscapes
unfold outside the bus
as two widows embrace
the fresh experiences
they view together through the window.

But conversations
are laden with reflections
of other journeys
remembered from a time
when sorrow was a stranger
and loneliness an alien land.

Reactions to new events
are tinted by knowledge
of what might have been
had four faces been mirrored
in the bus window
instead of two.

TRAVEL

Farming

A company of lonely labourers encircles
the globe, one with the land they nurture.

Fences, wire or wood, stone or stump,
hedge of hemlock, define the farmer's labour.
Furrows are turned on pampas,
prairie, mesa and mountainside.
Seeds are planted in paddies
and dyked ditch-encircled fields.
Hay is forked, mist-laden
on wires strung across valleys.
Brittle stacks border quarter sections
and bales fill barn lofts.
Grains are scythed from small
stone bordered plots
while stooks dot alpine pockets.

Around the world farmers anxiously
watch the skies while fighting
nature with science and folklore.
They all finger swollen heads of grain
and smile contented with their labour
or weep for lost crops
downed by overabundant rains
or thinned by drought.

Separated by custom, language and distance
they are one in their solitudes.

A Bus Tour

We come together within our steel cocoon
strangers from foreign lands.
Our tentative forays into intimacy
are strengthened by shared experiences,
traded books, leisurely conversations,
breathtaking landscapes and long lineups.

When the bus door opens for the last time
we'll disperse, wrapped in common memories.
Yet we have touched each other,
shared ourselves, and widened our perspectives.
Pieces of each of you cling to me
and I have grown through knowing you.

TRAVEL

Camping Memory

Rolls of thunder rend the sky and lightning
flashes push torrents of rain bent on
destruction toward our summer paradise.

Our circle of tents huddles in the meadow
slack against the darkling winds of
night that close on sleeping campers.

Rain, driving like hungry cheetahs, pushes
against the billowing canvas and drowsy
we leaders anticipate an arduous fight with

nature. Don rubber boots. Wrap towels
round our necks. Throw heavy army surplus
ponchos over our heads. Shove sou'wester

hats on tousled hair and grab flashlights.
Shake them on while we shiver with dark
memories in anticipation of the crashing

fury awaiting us. Wrestling freed tent
flaps we leave the fragile security of
canvas that would be airborne and set off

around the circle of tents; a trio heads
right and one left. We work silently
for the fury of the night precludes talk.

One of us heads to the fastened door of the
tent and pokes her head in to calm the fears
of little campers and help them stay dry.

Two of us start down the sides of the tent
testing each guy line. Water streams from
our faces. Flashlights useless in the deluge

are shoved in our boots. Terrain memorized.
While lightning hunts us we move carefully.
Sight is superfluous. Years of handling canvas

let us gauge the tautness of the rope. Wicked
winds love loose canvas and push and pull and
shake until it collapses. Slamming rains

want tight canvas to wrest pegs from the ground
and rip the weft of woven security. Test the guy
line. Move the toggle. Work one on each side of

the tent sensing in the pelting rain and roaring
winds what our partner is doing. All tents checked.
All campers calm with gear not touching the canvas.

We meet in the middle of the meadow oblivious
of the storm that seeks revenge around us.
We stay outside and survey in lightning's

streaks of challenge, the worried but secure
tents. No sleep for us. Too exhilarated.
Too wet. Too tense. Too vigilant.

We form a circle within the circle
wet hands hugging wetter shoulders and
stepping ever faster in slippery boots

We splash new deep rivulets of frenzy under
our ponchos on clothes already soaked
and lift our faces to the pelting rain

to sing defiance to the raging tempest.
Hiding our fears we dance primordial chants.
Victors—for now.

TRAVEL

Walking Through History

As one of the hungry horde
of tiered pencil-weaving robots,
I listened to the cadences
of wisdom from behind the lectern
as lecturers stratified history.

Thick tomes complicated the story.
Lexicons of facts and figures
removed any romance
from the disconnected pictures
I struggled to assimilate.

Then I traveled through Europe.

While surveying the small huddle
of houses with appended barns,
I heard the galloping hordes
bent on terror and destruction
and the shrieking warriors
who swooped to meet them.

While viewing monastery ruin
I wandered past ancient crypts,
glimpsed distant empty caves,
and heard monks' scratching quills,
plainsong from the chapel,
and rustling robes in the cloisters.

While walking cathedral ruins
I prayed in ancient sanctuaries
replete with tablets to the famous,
heard homilies and canticles,
saw footsteps of myriad communicants,
and smelled the flowers of a thousand years.

Supplication to the Sun

Elusive god, sleeping
under thick cloud covers
you send rain nightmares
and torrential winds
to dampen our world.

We would see your face!

What supplications will entice
you to throw off thunder
and grace us with warmth and light?
Tell us the ritual dances
lost to generations we can step
to tickle you awake.

Impatiently we wait to perform
the rites of worship.
With covered eyes and oiled body
in suitable unclothed state
we'll stretch prone in silent awe
if only we can see you again.

TRAVEL

Heard While Touring Europe

At sidewalk cafes on cobble stone streets amid medieval
architecture
The coffee is cold.
> *Where's the ice water?*
> *I don't see the butter.*

In walled towns whose ramparts talk two thousand years
Look at the price—much cheaper at home.
> *Why can't they speak English!*
> *The tour cost too much.*
>> *I know it's the Mediterranean and it's July*
>> *but why is it so hot?*

Near hectares of vineyards at wineries famous around
the world
> *I've seen caves at home, these can't be as good.*

In hotels in the centre of cities with throngs of pilgrims
The room is too small.
> *This hotel is too old.*
>> *Where is the air conditioning?*
>>> *—they promised air conditioning.*

Complainers cover the globe.

Waiting.

Zurich, Amsterdam,
Vienna, Reykjevik,
Oslo, Dusseldorf,
Brussels, Paris,

Electronic board
lists exotic places.
Planes seek the sky.

12:20 last call,
14:30 wait in lounge,

Just blinking yellow lights
on T.V. screens side-by-side
while I sit, waiting for

16:20   Istanbul

green numbers, blue names,
yellow boarding information
bustles across the screen
as transit passengers
respond to Heathrow's summons.

Until numbers and letters
beckon me to seek clouds,
adventure is a dream.

TRAVEL

Water Music

Surf around the world
speaks the same language.
At Ketchican, Nanaimo and Vancouver
at St John's, Peggy's Cove and Halifax
on the coasts of France, Spain and Portugal
in Barbados, Finland and Thunder Bay
in lakes, seas, oceans and coves
waves form, build and crest
to crash white roils that tumble
to massage sand and rocks
then fall to form again.
A continuous refrain.

Always a four part chorus
voices singing in harmony
the message of sun, wind and rain
of slow soft breezes
or form a discordant choir with booming bass
orchestrating a storm provoked gale.

Climate's cacophony or serenity
articulates a universal tongue.

THE AMERICAS

CARIBBEAN

Second Sitting

Grackles with sleek ebony bodies
shimmering rainbows in the sun
perch on the backs of chairs
at empty tables. Fixing diners
with bright yellow eyes
they whine their demands
"my turn" "my turn."
Wispy breezes of Barbados
play around the restaurant.
Dropping crumpled napkins
diners saunter toward the beach.
 Grackle, saucy sentinel for second sitting
 calls his ravenous family on the rafters
 flies from his perch on the nearby chair
 to the table ravaged by lunch for four.
 Tails folded for balance
 They search crumpled linen
 for tasty scraps. Lunch at last.
 No squawking, time is short.

 No squabbling, there's enough for all.
 Grandfather scorns plain bread
 grasps the muffin with both feet
 tears tasty morsels with black beak.
 Youngster, family optimist, flies
 with toast larger than he is
 seeking solitude for gluttony.
Finally waiters end the feast,
clear the table, remove the last crumb.
Grackles retire to empty chairs
eye the neat tables
await their next course.

March Paradise

Magic carpets bring winter refugees
to cocoons of summer paradise.
Warm sands, murmuring waters
light breezes and hot sun
spin threads of numb comfort.
Walls of mindlessness
thickened by the ministrations
of unobtrusive Bajans
create our isolation.

In town under the same sun
angry ebony women march together.
A cappella shouts cut light breezes—
        STOP THE VIOLENCE
and frame placards of protest—
        FAMILY ABUSE IS A CRIME
Cries for peace plead for equality—
in an unrealized paradise.

CARIBBEAN

Cleaning the Pool
        (for Basil)

While the hum of the vacuum
softly caresses the Caribbean air,
Basil stands beside the pool,
responsibility printed on his T shirt.
Slowly he moves the cleaner
back and forth
            back and forth
                        back and forth
across the plunging concrete
while his shimmering ebony shadow

grasps the shining pipe that straightens
as it leaves the water.

The hose, bound at both ends,
slithers in waves below the surface
keeping lethargic time with the passing
cleaner who swings a brown frond
obliterating last night's revelry.
Mourning doves complain
over the murmur of the lapping sea.
As early towel-shrouded tourist
reclines beside the pool
waiting for her morning swim.
The security guard wanders from the beach,
eyes alert for strangers.

Still the vacuum sweeps slowly.
No grain of sand escapes.
Every flower and leaf is caught—
back and forth
      back and forth
            back and forth
impervious to the purple blossoms
that climb the tree beside the pool,
flutter down and float
on the water to claim the first
morning swim.

CARIBBEAN

Tortola   B.V.I.

Cane Garden Beach
green mountain sides
slide to ripples of white sand
hot bright cove curls protectively
inward with arms of green
blue sea slips toward hot shore
rolling slowly to caress the beach
beyond Drake River flows
steadily by from one island to another
ignoring a cradle of serenity.

Just One

Tropic breezes waft
floral scents and sunny warmth
to draw stress from my pores
infused from the cold work world
Content, I float on the sun's rays
from pool to beach to balcony
A dream within an island paradise
At day's end I drift toward the dining room
        JUST ONE
shoulders tense I reply
        YES, I'M ALONE
Seated calmly, I fill my vision
with sand and sea my heart
with calypso and smile at the waiter
        IS SOMEONE ELSE COMING?
back muscles knot
        NO, I'M ALONE
Order taken, ordeal over
I search for serenity while
smiling and nodding to my neighbours
A bus boy arrives to remove the
other place setting
        A LONER I SEE
Justifiable homicide might just exist

CARIBBEAN

Catamaran

A dancer, she moves
to maestro wind's baton.
The jib and mains'l absorb
the beat of the sea,
pale and true blue, that twines
around the stepping hull.

At anchor she swings a lullaby
while white waves waltz the sands,
palms sway and bow in harmony.
She holds a pose long seconds
before continuing her ballet.

Beach Towels

Beach towels are sentient beings.
Before dawn they drape themselves
over lounge chairs on beaches
around the world.
Rows of them crowd the sands
and watch the sea hour after hour
with corners flapping pleasure.
Sometimes, at dawn, or noon, or sunset,
people, who don't know any better,
flop on top of the towels
obstructing their view
and diverting warm breezes.
Patiently towels wait, until intruders leave
when they once more own the beach.

After sunset they mysteriously disappear.
Do not mourn, they'll return before sunrise.

CARIBBEAN

Watch Watching in Barbados

Watches are to look at
actual time not important
it's minutes until or since
that drive watch watchers.

How many minutes
until spa appointment?
How many seconds
until store opens?

In hot countries,
there are few watch-watchers.
Native walkers stroll deadline free.
Store owners yawn to open tardy doorlocks.
Notice at resort restaurant says
diners are seated and served at 6:30.
Watch-watchers arrive at 6:30—or earlier.
First person seated at 6:45—or later.

No staff member is a watch watcher.
They don't wear Seiko or Gucci,
Rolex or Timex.
No cuckoos call the hours;
no pendulums punctuate minutes.

How come, if they never watch a watch,
They're never early?

Church in Yaxcaba Mexico

16th century saint
on the north wall,
framed in blue and gold
bas-relief columns
that are framed in twining
garlands of red and blue.

In front a rough-hewn
wooden cross draped
with aging white gauze
with flower rainbow
heavily embroidered
along its length.

In front a simple glass vase
filled with water holds
two yellow rose buds
beaded with dew.

Tourists tramp the aisles
gawk at colonial architecture
and gaze at altar and reredos
their empty voices echo off the wall.

Someone
worshipped this morning.

MEXICO

Mayan Ruins

Jungles reclaimed early civilizations.
Trees and vines buried heaps of rubble,

vestiges of walls, life stories and cultures.
Stone gods scattered on the jungle floor
interred under earth and roots,
are all forgotten.

Almost forgotten.
The carver's work peeked
through encroaching vegetation.
History of ancestors skimmed
the surface of Mayan memories.

> Ruins were discovered.
> Archeologists dug.
> Builders reconstructed.
> Historians pondered the pieces.

Chichen-Itza, Uxmal, Yaxchilan,
Palenque, Monte Alban, Tulum.
Sites of successful civilizations
fill the Yucatan Peninsula
spreading north into Mexico
and south through Latin America.

Stories emerge from the sand.
Rubble rises again as walls,
rooms, stairs, and statues.
Stone gods stand mute.
Playing fields await the game.
Stone serpents glow in equinox sun.

Gradually time is reversed,
yesterday's genius walks today.

Tourist in Mayaland.

Rain God,
carved on temple ruins,
turn your eyes to me.
Shake your ear lobes.
Gnash your stone teeth.

Pour your rain upon our heads.
Scientists desert for drier sites but
we will not leave! We came to learn!
Send your torrents, still we listen,
gaze in awe, click cameras
and drip our way toward the bus.

USA, NEW HAMPSHIRE

York Harbor, New Hampshire

Boats dot the sun-drenched bay
like teddy bears in a toy box
waiting for the school bell.
Sweet rustling shore grasses
mingle with the salty kelp spray
to tingle the nostrils.
Laughing voices waft across the water
calling to the slow tide
that tugs the sails at anchor.
Lifted motors kiss the sea
like race horses, impatient
for the starting gate.
Playfulness strains against
the reins of serenity.

Honolulu–U.S. Arizona Memorial

"Remember Pearl Harbor"
emblazoned on ball cap visors
engraved on key chains
stenciled on T-0shirts
Remember, remember, remember

Remember Troy, Armageddon, Waterloo
Remember Gallipoli, Ypres, Vimy Ridge
Remember Dachau, Leningrad, Coventry
Remember, Rwanda, South Africa, Iraq

Remember swords, rifles, artillery, bombs
Remember valor, fear, mourning, hate

Why do we remember?
So we can exact revenge, harbor hate, learn war
or so we can feel compassion, practise peace, learn love

So we can create communities of abundance
from fractured relationships.

USA, HAWAII

U.S. Arizona Memorial

Water laps a lullaby at concrete base
Whispers walk the overview of chaos
Soft breezes wash still faces caught in memory
One single-engine plane scrapes blue sunlit sky
on an overpass below the clouds
Launch drone silenced on return to shore
Quietly, reverently, we remember.

Yet surrounding the peace we remember
Bombers, in row after row scream overhead
Battleships explode, belch black smoke
and sink in the roiling harbor waters
Airfields of huddled planes blow apart
Sirens pierce the chaos as men and women
scramble to live, to save lives, to die.

We mourn anew alienation and hate
and catch our breath to see them still.

After Act I

audience assembles before light dims
crowds the beach and faces western stage
slowly sun sinks behind purple mountain

when last blush of orange orb disappears
audience turns and walks away
from longest running show on earth

with an almost empty house Act II begins
from off stage sun flings her brilliant
shimmering crimsons yellows tangerines

she paints clouds sky and beach in changing hues
gives her all to small remaining audience
who stands mesmerized until night's curtain falls

USA, HAWAII

Couples in a Restaurant.

Arms folded, heads facing away from each other
each shrinks into self, alone together.

Fingers, eyes and voices touch across the table
one handed, knives forgotten, they eat together.

One talks, retelling "I" stories, while the other
sits eyes glazed, smile frozen, knife clenched.

Tentative hands touch knees beneath the table
shy eyes smile through simple conversation.

One complains to maitre d', waiter, partner
of table, food, service. Companion cringes.

Conversation flows, condiments anticipated
faces smile as new memories relived in laughter.

Communication

Bus driver/guide stops his spiel
competing one-sided conversation
becomes audible   a tourist calling home.

A couple sit in a restaurant
silently   ignored   she eats
dinner ignored   he talks to cell phone

Nature dazzles with rainbow over mountain
Business woman, one hand on briefcase
one hand to her ear, sees only metallic voice.

Young couple walk the beach holding hands
two cell phones active, both talk loudly
Are they talking to each other?

What's next? bedroom? dance floor?
When did we lose the other four senses?

USA, SOUTH CAROLINA

Myrtle Beach Morning

sky is splashed pink from the coming sunrise
and feather clouds stolen from the gulls
toss wisps of white above the sea.
Sleeping waters stir with the new day
and their little white slashes wipe
the sand clean of the memory of gulls
that walk the shore, quiet as the day awakens.

Fire in Yellowstone Park
         (August 1988)

I remember exploding geysers
and bubbling sulphur pools
the drive beside canyons
gouged by rushing waters;
peaceful forest campsites
images of self discovery.

Now angry flames sweep the park
roar through the underbrush
and claw indiscriminately skyward.
Mindless devastation swipes away
the echoes of rustling leaves
browsing moose and laughing campers.

Dying lodgepole pines spew cones
to seed the smoking ground.
New trees rooted in destruction
will push their way through ash
to grow tenaciously near fireweed
with promises of life renewed.

USA, WASHINGTON

Holiday Pictures—1
Washington State

Happiness shines
in our faces
as we turn
from the mountains
and face the camera.

Warm western breezes,
chattering squirrels
and sweet scented blooms
are awakened from
my memory.

I feel the warmth
of your body
and hug the touch
of your arm
around my back.

I see the mountains
encircling
our highway refuge.
They shelter us
with serenity.

The frozen forms
swim from the page
and I am there,
transformed
with happiness.

EUROPE

ENGLAND

London Church
"Enter, rest and pray all who are weary."

Chiseled in grime above the door
the words whisper to all
who scurry past this downtown church
in England's largest city.

Look below the optimistic summons.
The massive black door is closed,
padlocked with chains of finality
that mock the cold stone message.

Pedestrians rush toward the underground.
Black taxis and red busses
play out their set dances in the road.
All are oblivious to the decaying building.

Paper trash, pushed by the wind, swirls against the door.

London Taxi

Youthful dowager
impeccably groomed
but masking individuality,
your yellow lights wink
at me after the play.

Patient with surging crowds
and a plethora of coaches
you manoeuver around
crowded streets, roundabouts
and millions of tourists.

Driven by a philosopher
who will discuss the world
or the weather on cue,
your squealing brakes
deposit me at the hotel door.

And it's all done efficiently
on the wrong side of the road!

ENGLAND

Cities in the Night

Pools of light stab silence
accenting still, dark streets.
People sleep behind locked doors.
Underground has ceased its roar.
London taxies have escorted
sleepy tourists to their hotels.

When I last parted hotel curtains
to greet the winking lights of night
Toronto was alive with marching bands
as carefree engineering students
snaked through insomniac vehicles
and serenaded nocturnal wanderers.

How old must cities be
to cloak night with silence?

Dining Room in Our London Hotel

Pillars imitating Greek splendour
ring the chamber. They are supported
by ornately molded high ceilings
with coved sections encircling
huge glistening chandeliers.

Two massive stone fireplaces
topped with shimmering mirrors
encased in elaborately carved frames
reflect each other's splendour
from across the opulent room.

Tables placed in clusters
are resplendent with starched linen
richly decorated silver and glassware
and served by white-jacketed waiters
with soft voices and deep bows.

The chef oversees the buffet
in white-clothed simplicity.
Only the height of his hat
stretched to imitate the columns
speaks of his prestigious post.

Carefully orchestrated comfort
from a more leisurely era
is interrupted by the beeps
of the computer in the corner
calculating the charges.

ENGLAND

Shadowlands

Moonlit London street casts faint shadows
as we leave the darkened theatre—where
we lived with two who formed one silhouette
in a world they neither knew nor sought.
Reason lost to passion.
Logic fallen to tenderness.
Marquee's artificial light seeks street lamps
and traffic beams to force us to the night.
Reality is not in midnight London neon
nor in flickering moon shadows
but in the joy of love and cruelty of death
revealed behind the footlights a moment ago.

Taxi stops. Driver asks, "Where to Gov.?"
I cannot voice ethereal longing, so name
our hotel and crowd the cab with shadows.

Glendalough, Ireland

St. Kevin's monastery
built between two lakes
in a hollow in the hills
welcomed monks and pilgrims
from the first millennium of faith

now crumbled cathedral
small stone church
mysterious round tower
ancient tilted tombstones
nestle in meadow and forest

while the swish of monks' robes
whispers of early worshipers
wails of heavy-laden mourners
and compline prayers in vaulted haven
echo in my bones

SWITZERLAND

Rhein Falls

The rushing sunlit cascade
is impervious to the world it sustains.
Cherished chalets climb the mountain slopes
and chiming cattle seek the peaks.
Safe cities host peacemakers while
citizen soldiers tunnel for security.
Tourist dollars are enticed
by chocolate and cuckoo clocks.

Happy accordions, beckoning yodels
harmonious bells and dancing voices
join the music of the waterfall.

A plethora of tour coaches
disgorge camera-clicking pilgrims
who imitate water's mindless quest.

Fields of Sunflowers

Masses of yellow
symbols of happiness
stretch from wheat to clover
fields and turn toward the sun
while rooted in the soil of France.
Nod to the coaches and caravans
who flaunt their mobility.
Smile for the cameras
that capture their radiance
but stay—sway the dance
of breeze and sun.

Harvest cannot destroy
the memory of summer's
golden symphony.

FRANCE

Rivers of France

The rivers of France shape the land
on their relentless passage to the sea.

They comb the countryside outlining
wheat and sunflowers   define oceans
of vineyards on eastern slopes and knit
the skeins of valleys and hills.

They murmur through cities and around
chateaux oblivious to aliens who sail
tides   cradle on their walled shores
or lurch roaring engines mindlessly.

They gurgle onward   reflect magnificent
stone and steel stretched to pierce the sky
flirt under bridges that carried Caesar's armies
flow past the homeless in shadowed sleep.

They move silently amid cannons of conflict
and are diverted often for our whims
but always they meander unforgiving
unforgetting   seeking the sea.

The Loire, Seine and Somme
the Marne, Rhine and Rhone
define the soul of France .

Atonement Day—Rouen France

Narrow cobblestone street
funnels pilgrim masses
steadily, inexorably from
Notre Dame Cathedral
to the place of St. Joan's
burning. As at Canterbury,
Jerusalem or Mecca we
plod toward spiritual history.

What draws us on? I hope
we seek atonement for
the witch hunt mentality that
lit the fire at St. Joan's feet.

But in cafes and on corners
I hear conversations
about refugees, immigrants,
aboriginals, other races,
colours, religions and know
we still strike the match to burn
those we do not understand.

FRANCE

Omaha Beach—Normandy France

Before me
smooth sun-kissed sands
wet by softly rippling waters
are barely disturbed by breezes
that kiss their surface
then travel up the bluff to sing
in harmony with rustling trees.

A Carillon tolls
hymns of yesterday that pool
toward waves of white crosses,
each covering two comrades.
Parents hush skipping children.
Voices whisper. Feet tread softly.
Hearts hold awe at the sacrifice
of over nine thousand who fought
for freedom and found their peace
the same day.

On that day
staccato roar of opposing artillery
raged over nature's harmonies.
Water roiled with landing craft
tossing hordes of young soldiers
onto sands pocked by guns,
littered with wounded and dead.
Soldiers screaming courage
during a baptism to savage battle
splashed toward eternity.

Sidewalk Café

Small tables, simple chairs
clustered under bright umbrellas
huddle around a store front
"Un Perrier,"
"Un café de creme grand s'il vous plait."
A respite from cathedrals, postcards,
patisseries and shops with specialties
of the region.

Time to stop and take a breath
amid medieval buildings and watch
other visitors search for one more
memento, cheap but good quality,
to stuff in the suitcase tonight.

We sip the surface of France
but where is her soul?

FRANCE

Mont Saint Michel—France

We cluster in the nave.
A robed Benedictine monk
carries a strobe light across the choir
while the guide tells of crypts, chapels,
refectory, cloister, guest rooms.

We remember our tour of centuries
layered in stone, space and light,
stories of peace and war,
dreams and miracles, of monks
chained by religious belief who hosted
myriad searching pilgrims, and of prisoners
chained by political expedience
through eons of democracy.

Now monks have returned.
We pilgrims climb the crowded street
past small stores of souvenirs and food,
scale the stairs to spired skies,
to search for meaning in our breathless world.

Riviera—France

Twisting mountain roads
overlook a blue sea where
boats with large motors
and tall-masted ships scamper at play.

White villas cling one above
the other and huddle side by side
with red tile roof and tropic
greenery to define their privacy.

I look for Cary Grant to disembark
from a cruise ship with Deborah Kerr
or to hurl twisting roads in a convertible.
with saucy, young, Grace Kelly.

This land for the rich is
a story book of movies and tabloids.
Yet I walk the palace public rooms
shuffle past Princess Grace's tomb
hear the roar of tires that hurdle us
through tunnels and past hillsides.
I stretch toward the coach window
to glimpse cavorting sea craft.

I'll carry the legends into tomorrow.

FRANCE

Sharing
(Church in St. Paul de Vence, France)

stone masons   wood carvers   iron workers
candle makers   painters and master builders
have toiled through the centuries to God's glory

this modest monument to faith is dark and still
lit by sun from the East and candles
of prayer and petition that flicker in the gloom

this is not Reims or Paris but through the years
its simple splendour has echoed with parishioners
who knelt in fear of war and to laud peace

stood in exultation and celebration
bent in overwhelming grief and humility
and sang in prayer   praise and thanksgiving

sit   be still   share the litany of a million masses
share faith with saints and angels of a thousand years
share God with those who came before and will follow

be still   know God within this edifice and your heart

Masks

Main streets in some French towns
are lined with untended facades.
Paint chipped wonky shutters
fashion window mysteries;
black-streaked stone walls
crowd busy sidewalks.

But narrow one-story arches
or scarred wooden doors
between unyielding disguises
are passageways to serenity.

Arbours of scented rainbows
cradle grass-hugging benches.
Chairs and tables circle fountains
that whisper peace.

A quiet world. A private world.
Ignoring—denying—muffling—
the bustle of trade and tourists.

GERMANY

Images of Dachau
Concentration Camp 1933-1945

PRELUDE   Truth was eroded by book burnings.
As new laws stole personal freedoms
a succession of scapegoats
were herded and harried by neighbours
who buried the sanctity of life.

THEN   Desperate cries and enslaving roars
framed the rows of crowded bunk houses.
Hanging trees ended uncertain life
and hungry crematoriums sent
foul smelling smoke belching toward heaven.

NOW   Museum images recall the twelve year tragedy
and create shock waves to the consciousness
of tourists who walk the concrete corridors.
Silently, they approach the memorials.
Cold clean ovens leave dirty memories.

POSTLUDE United Nations strive for harmony:
stockpiled weapons preserve an empty peace;
the innocent die from terrorism
struck in the name of nationalism;
and the free call for censorship.

Waiting in Lisbon

Arc of tan taxies hugs the curb
seven— bumper to bumper
with central eyes darkly waiting.

Umbrella capped drones bustle past
seek familiar buses.

Still, tan cars wait. Patiently. Still.
Soon streets will fill with tourists.
Taxis will waken. Lights will light busy.

New eyes in an old city wait
to breathe Lisbon's ambience.

PORTUGAL

Portugal Shore
Between Sintra and Cascais

Heaps of limestone bathed in spray are carved
by encroaching surf as it tumbles to shore.

Free-formed sculptures along the coast line
evolve slowly by incessant white foam
that curls landward then pulls out to sea.

Sun pushes through cloud crowds
to sparkle murmuring surf alive

Fluid blues, greens and whites splash
mottled grey, black and brown rock
and join with the wind-drone to create
an angry cantata pulsing through the hours.

Monument to the Discoveries
Lisbon, Portugal.

Figures stand
kneel, crouch, sit
one behind another
down two sides of
stylized stone caravel.
Each holds symbol of expertise
writer, poet, historian
cartographer, mother
prince, explorer, navigator.
All support Prince Henry —
practical visionary.

A nation peered beyond their shores
to mythically dangerous seas—away
away from home, away from safety
to the unknown—
coast of Africa, southern cape,
Indian Ocean, India, seas beyond.
They found new sails and spices
different foods, culture, philosophies

Western world changed the east.
Eastern lands influenced the west.
World community expanded.
World shrank.

PORTUGAL

People Watching in Coimbra, Portugal

Medieval street. Steep, narrow, pedestrian walkway
paved with small irregular yellow bricks.
Shops' wares spill from both sides
almost meeting in the middle.
Sidewalk café at the delta—
metal table holds steaming espresso
and almond pastry, chairs cradle
midmorning people-watchers.

Women, clothed in bottom-hugging
bell bottoms that top high-heeled boots
and short waist-gripping jackets
in leather or suede, stride
precariously and purposefully
to somewhere.
Men, in black-suits, white shirts,
tight ties, and shining leather shoes,
broadcast their devotion to work
with scuffed brown leather brief cases
as they walk resolutely, impervious to the crowd.

Camera-strapped tourists stroll
up hill and back down
from postcards to shoes
from jewellery to T-shirts
from ATM to pottery or leather
gawking, buying and clicking
in one more historic city.

Languages, lyrical and guttural
staccato the air.
One woman, in red skirt and peasant blouse
with back straight and arms swinging,
punctuates the crowd with a large wicker basket
full of embroidered white linens
balanced on her head.

PORTUGAL

Guadaina River
separating Portugal from Spain

Wide, quiet brown river runs slowly to the sea.
Hills rise on both sides; one replicates the other.
Near the water— low vegetation covers wild slopes
where ruins, tumble precariously.
Farther away, crops terrace hills
hug modern barns and houses.
Two shores, two flags, two countries.

Modern suspension bridge stretches
from Spanish city to Portuguese town.
Gulls soar freely.
Clouds scud across open skies.
Sun and rain shower both shores
and the river meanders between.
One natural community, one world.

Storm in a Market Town
Quarteira, Portugal

Massive black clouds above the sea
pour rain upon the roiling waves.

Soon, sun, white cloud wisps
and hot summer breeze
are pushed down the coast
as angry wet winds assault the town.
Market stalls hide wares
under stone-weighted plastic,
café awnings crack staccato,
chairs scurry across the brick road,
dust and debris swirl on the beach.
Dripping tourists laughingly
sit in captured chairs and call for coffee.
Dusk descends early.

Suddenly, wind subsides, awnings relax,
sand stills the imprints of the wind,
coffee cups empty, bills are paid,
tables are cleared and wiped.
Stalls, in meandering rows of
T-shirts, deep-fried donuts,
leather purses, belts, jackets,
hand-painted pottery, embroidered linens,
hand-knitted sweaters, key chains and postcards
emerge as wet folded plastic disappears.
Human statues appear from nowhere,
Guatemalan musicians ripple the air,
hawkers again bellow bargains
and beckon Euro-rich gawkers.
Dusk has disappeared, until later.

PORTUGAL

Walking the Beach in Portugal

sea and wind unite to sing
their praises to the sun
fishermen scoop beneath sand
for shell fish deposited by the tide
children play in gentle breakers

as parents watch with smiling eyes
we trudge on   slowly race the tide
eyes dart catch bites of beauty
ears sing whispers of sand and sea
feet push against hard wet sand

ahead   behind seaside hotel
shopkeepers awaken stores
fishermen gut and hang the day's catch
old men sitting in the sun settle in to quaff
day's activities and comment on them

the pier is quiet   too late for fishermen
too early for tourist hordes
café awnings open a yawn
coffee pots bubble in anticipation
a new day begins

Holy Week in Guimaraes, Portugal

Granite church from the middle ages
stands proudly in the valley.
Its spires pierce a hillside of vineyards
and clusters of white, red-roofed houses.

Crowding the valley square
golden-tiled apartments shelter
tulip beds that parade red and yellow
from church to fountain-centred traffic circle.

Mauve pennants, each with sorrowing Jesus,
chant holy week to bustling cars and strolling people.
Mauve crosses draped in white,
flutter above—beckoning our souls.

SPAIN

La Rambla—Barcelona, Spain

Sangria-sipping elderly ladies rest
weary feet at sidewalk café; watch crowds
stroll by flower stalls, news stands, canvas boutiques,
hawkers, portrait artists and human statues.
Families, tourist groups, and solitary walkers
weave paths, shoulders nearly touching, telling
their stories with expression, voice, and posture.

Police trio, night sticks prominent
meander with creased pants, shiny shoes.
Their heads search the masses for shifting eyes,
familiar faces, slippery hands.

Child pulls against a T-shirt neck
eyes bugged, tongue lolling.
Father holds the ribbed neck
like a leash, sets his own pace.

Young tot in crackling starched
shirt and tie, hair slicked smooth
holds mother's hand, becomes
tidy extension of her tidy arm.

Boy, wheedles, coaxes, walks backwards
head swivels from parents
to balloon man waving wares his way.
Family turn to smiling merchant.

Older boy of six with balloon hat
gives younger stranger a passing wink.
Both grin as money and balloons
change hands.

Police meet three colleagues, one shrugs
his shoulders, one spreads empty hands.
They chat, bodies relaxed but always
eyes shift back and forth, working.

Spain

Olive groves line valleys,
climb gentle hills.
Narrow cobblestone streets
meld centuries of history.
Tooting car braves hordes
of tourists to twist and climb,
brushing buildings with air.

> Cathedrals cradle gold and silver
> within sweeping gothic spires.
> Mosaics whisper ancient subjugation.
> Artists and architects story the past,
> colour today and shape tomorrow.

Shuttered shops greet deserted
afternoon sidewalks, then open
when evening crowds— families,
widowed crones, and sidewalk-owning
clumps of gesturing men—stroll
the streets in waning light.

> Guitars mix east and west to form
> haunting melodies. Castanets
> click as rigid bodies focus tapping feet.
> Impressions—sips of wine
> intoxicate as the coach moves on.

Norge Foss

Snow embossed mountains
are silent in winter stillness

Spring sun urges snow melt
to yawn, stretch and slowly waken
that rivulet deltas can mingle
and begin the push to the sea

Water falls down the mountains
cascades from rock to rock
trills against slate ledges
slaps like cymbals in rock forced splashes
fingers bass chords as rapids form
and rush a deep roar under bridges
to roil past protruding rocks
undercutting sharp turns
that send mist skyward

Water travels down, desperately down
always moving, gathers momentum
speeds urgently to the sea

Slowly   waters greet the fjords
that came from far oceans to meet them
They mingle in quiet contemplation

NORWAY

Mountains

I'm sure, in a past life
I knew a mountain.
In the Rockies or Laurentians
by alpine meadows or Norse fiords,
I am home.

I gulp visions of waterfalls
inhale the beauty of bird songs
stretch my mind to snowy peaks
and whisper with the waters
rushing to the sea.

Welcomed back by majesty
memories tickle my heart
and I am home again.

Norse Fiords

I seek the ancient Vikings
who tackled unknown waters
and wandered my home shores.

No oars sweep the sea.
No dragons pierce west.
But rugged mountains
frame the cold fiord
gulls play confidently
with capricious winds
and farmers struggle
to tame the mountain sides.

Though I traced their footprints
their hearts are strangers.
Each journey is a slice of time.
I garner my own meanings
among Norse fiords.

NORWAY

Lumbering in Norway

Dead trolls outline the fiords
but live ones drive
the noisy steel monsters
that rip the guts
out of mountain slopes.

*Troll are unseen creatures in Norway. When they get angry they
explode, and become rocks. Live ones can inhabit the bodies of
humans and make them do bad things like logging in the
mountains.*

Modern Vikings

Ten centuries ago
legendary Vikings, eager seekers
of unknown perils, left the fiords.
Today's brave encircle them
driving buses perched precariously
on pencils of twisting pavement
that hug the mountain slopes.

ASIA

RUSSIA

Russia, Today

beside a paint-chipped back door
stand two brooms
they rest on tiled alley
lean against red brick wall

one made of twigs
bound with binder twine
around a rough long handle
knot and stump enhanced
with two spots of sweat gleaming
and grimy with constant use

the other made of plastic
clean yellow bristles caught in blue mold
pristine green broomstick
shiny   straight   smooth
gripping hands wait for strange
unfamiliar feeling to disappear

both sweep the gutters
by St. Isaac's Cathedral

Sergiev Posad, Russia

in St. Sergius Monastery
black-robed bearded monks
stride among blue and gold
onion-spired churches

inside   a reredos
of gold-framed icons
tells ancient stories
incense swirls
'round massive pillars
supplicants light candles
chant an ancient liturgy
walk slowly past priests
silent tourists watch in awe
tinged with sanctity

outside in the courtyard
beneath richly painted arches
the faithful fill jugs of pottery and plastic
at the sacred fountain

eleven churches revive an ancient religion
three hundred monks work   study   worship
and walk again among the laity and curious

RUSSIA

Russia

wide car-clogged roads
tourist buses snail along
Moscow is ahead

> *Winter snows blow horror*
> *Napoleon's army stalls*
> *Moscow is saved*

a portable stage
erected in Red Square
for Paul McCartney

> *Rows of marching soldiers*
> *Follow tanks and armored cars*
> *Stalin's May Day square*

people stroll the mall
past Gap Benneton   McDonalds
cells phones at their ears

> *Long lines of women*
> *Inch for bread from empty stores*
> *Communist society*

myriad parks abound
with clones of westerners
free to make choices

> *Gorky Street, Kremlin*
> *Siberia camps of exile*
> *Stuff of books and films*

Gallipoli

Blood red poppies bob nearby
yellow flowers mirror the sun
hill of death covered
with green forgetfulness.
Granite graves carved with names,
regiment, date and words of peace
memories pocked by years as friends grow old.
The restless sea rolls blue murmurs
toward our dead.

Pristine trenches still and clean
shout in the silence of dirty fear
as men far from home
challenged faceless defenders.
Bullets and artillery exchanged
for reasons far removed
from hearts stopped by lead.

On hills dotting the landscape
cloned monuments, rows of bones
Turk and Aussie, Kiwi and Canuck
groan to a new generation.

TURKEY

Fashion Show

Tourist bus empties at the Leather Factory.
Herded inside, apple tea in hand
we watch models strut the runway.
Skimpily clad girls hug wafer thin leather coats
that sway like silk and shimmer brightly.
Men in jeans and T-shirts look macho
in jackets geared for motor cycle or business.
Eyes sparkle, smiles beckon,
hands touch fashion features sensuously.

If male models wore pants as short
and tight as their female friends
we could practice leering too.

Music

Long pool, blue shimmering water
swimmers slice lengths rhythmically
behind   another pool splashes
laughter on child-filled water slides.
Parents sit around umbrella clad tables.
Electronic frenzy pumps mindless
energy loudly into yellow heat.
Holiday hysteria propels vacationers
to driving, swirling, incessant restlessness.

Where is birdsong?
Where are swaying palms and gentle breezes?
Where are quiet coves of rock and sand
with murmuring waves to trickle ideas
through our slowing beating hearts?

Where is the time to cherish ourselves
each other and our world? To dream?
To rest? To love? To find renewal?

Keep cacophony pumping. Keep minds closed.
Keep limbs whirling and voices shouting.
If the treadmill stops—

We might find ourselves...
and each other.

TURKEY

Languid fluid

Motor is still, anchor chain creaks softly,
voices call lazily from the deck.
Laughter flies across bulging waves.
Swimmers, free from our world
luxuriate in lapping salt sea.

They talk softly   share
Mediterranean splendour
ignore jesting hull-bound friends
not baptized with liquid diamonds
that swish blue over their limbs.

Adornment

one way street signs
stop lights around rotaries
flashing red at intersections
stuttering paint indicating lanes

in Turkey—only decoration—
all drivers demand right-of-way
with blaring horn and heavy foot.

Turkey — Europe and Asia.

Turkey is mountains, plains and seas
cities, villages and countryside—
an old woman selling her crocheted doilies
a young boy following tourists pleading
"Please lady, one dollar."

Turkey is haunting music, drumming,
story dances told in colourful costume,
sheaves and bales, sickles and combines
horse-drawn carts and clean busses
cave homes, skin tents and Hilton hotels.

Turkey is sesame seed buns, figs, dates and olives
peaches, apple tea, eggplant and cucumber
oil drenched zucchini in eye appealing buffets
of minted soups, goat's cheese, thick coffee,
lamb kebabs, and cayenne scrambled eggs.

Turkey is history tumbled on ancient plains
Hittite, Greek, Roman, Byzantine empires
early Christian churches, ancient mosques
tiled walks, chariot ruts, and Roman baths.
Myths, letters, wars—live still.

Turkey is contradictions, pushed by Ataturk
from sultan states to democracy.
Minarets broadcast daily prayers.
Mosque museums draw sock-clad pilgrims
and cities imitate London or Paris.

TURKEY

Mediterranean Waterfall
(Antalya, Turkey.)

Water hums a homecoming
song splashes downward
feels sun breezes
and hands in the air
plunges in swirling mist
toward sandstone rocks
protruding from the sea.

Like a pilgrim she rushes
fervently, plunging
in shimmering snow-like
drifts of ecstasy ever downward
where she muddles in mists
of mystery   home at last
home to the sea.

Turkey—Now and Then Mingle
(Iznik 1997 A.D.— Nicaea 325 A.D.)

circles of marigold magic
enclose bubbling fountains
that gurgle high water mass
then fall   to sprinkle sunlight
into cool blue pool

> *I believe in one God, the Father Almighty*
> *Maker of Heaven and earth.*
> *And of all things visible and invisible.*

down the street an imposing dome
is topped by a large untidy nest
stork rests on her flight south
watches the town awaken

> *And in one Lord Jesus Christ...*
> *Begotten of his Father before all worlds,....*
> *Very God of very God, Begotten not made.*

yellow bus spews forth tourists
St. Sophia first for Christ
then a mosque for Allah
now an edifice to dissension

> *Being of one substance with the Father;*
> *Who... was incarnate by the Holy Ghost*
> *of the Virgin Mary, And was made man....*

old men in wool shirts   vests   jackets   caps
stroll toward local sidewalk café
oblivious of impending heat
eager to tell stories   discuss   argue
about their city   their world—today

Index

Credits

The following poems have been published previously in the following publications:

Diviners:
   March Paradise, 1997

Inner Voices, Serengeti Press:
   Water Music

Journey With Grief:
   Reflections

Mostly Celebrations:
   Second Sitting; London Church; London Taxi;
   Dining Room in Our London Hotel,

The Tower :
   Second Sitting Vol. 40, #2;
   Dining Room in Our London Hotel Vol. 38, #2;
   Omaha Beach–Normandy France, Vol 43, #1;
   Sharing, Vol. 44. #2;
   Masks, Vol.45, #1;
   Church in Yaxcaba Mexico, Vol. 51, #1;
   People Watching in Coimbra, Portugal, Vol. 51, #2;
   Storm in a Market Town, Quarteira Portugal, Vol 51, #2;
   Turkey–Now and Then Mingle. Vol. 46, #2;
   Gallipoli, Turkey, Vol. 50, #2;

Reading Workbook Series, Tree House Press:
   Mayan Ruins, Grade 5; Farming, Grade 6:

Witness, Serengeti Press 2004:
   Remembrance Day
   Images of Dachau Concentration Camp, 1933-1945